Crossing
the Burnside Bridge

& OTHER POEMS

JANICE D. RUBIN

CIRQUE PRESS

Copyright © 2023 Janice D. Rubin

Published by

Sandra Kleven — Michael Burwell
3157 Bettles Bay Loop
Anchorage, AK 99515

CIRQUEJOURNAL@GMAIL.COM
CIRQUEJOURNAL.COM

Cover art Adobe Stock
Author photo by Nicole Taylor
Book Design by Kari Odden of Moontide Design

Print ISBN: 979-8-89145-357-9

For my first poetry critique group,
the *Let Them Eat Cake Poets*
and for my sisters, Barb and Sal

Table of Contents

III. Love and Transformation

I.

Voices Echoing Within

Young Woman Sage

—the Sower, personification of liberty
1850, Jean Francois Millet

She reads the sky as scripture
quotes the clouds
looks to the horizon
sows the fields
strides in the loam.

Holy gypsy, knows what is unknown
speaks without sound,
walks with the rhythm of the seasons
gathers suns for her pocket,
her eyes quiet and three seas blue.

A wet sheen from a green river stone
rests in her hand
for seconds, centuries
of speaking to her
in ancient sea rhythms.

Sacred forests, shadows of rain,
pale mystic cathedral spires all live
in silent meditation within her.
She holds a breath of summer in her lungs
a season of freedom on her tongue.

The Dashboard Saint

St. Roxie, the patron saint of women entrepreneurs
stands at attention on my dashboard with her beatific smile.
She wears a black blazer, a grey skirt just below the knee
sensible shoes painted on with precision
by some dedicated miniature buff.

Her vocation is my dashboard guide,
a mission she has accepted to spur me on.
She claims credit for a Buddhist prayer for the life force
to fully open, for potential to blossom
like a lotus in a muddy swamp.

St. Roxie stands on my dashboard
in her best and only business blazer
briefcase at her side, she faces
the vicissitudes of life unflinching,
the challenges of being in business for herself.

Her hair does not move, although there is texture.
Her parted coiffure is raised in places
making it as real as plastic can be.
She's a brave saint with a mission, a noble profile
and a prince valiant haircut.

Roxie of the dashboard,
not sanctioned by the Vatican or society,
she's working on acceptance.
St. Roxie takes the long-term view
on the highway of life with its bends and turns.

St. Roxie, a modern saint but not a martyr,
not St. Theresa of Avilla or St. Joan of Arc,
no sins of omission or sins of commission, only sins of ambition.
No complacency behind the headlights,
she drives on into the dark night.

GARGOYLE ON MOUNT PISGAH

Like a wicked winged gargoyle, I survey the mountainside
catch eddies, rise higher in the gyre.
Fierce winds graze my bare bones; I circle, soar, dive.

At the top of the mountain, gusts swell over
verdant shades of green and tan patched farmland,
stretched among red strawberry and tulip fields.

During the descent, down a steep trail
facing the wind, scattered purple flowers
remind me of your kisses.

Last summer we climbed these hills,
oak trees dispersed among tangled scotch broom,
yellow bushes woven amongst green velvet.

Hawks fly, drift, catch sun beyond illumination.
In the city below, blocks of granite pulse with August fever
opaque silver windows flash across the polis.

Fishing for Herring

That brilliant crisp morning
the sun rays skipped persuasively
over the sleeping pier.

Six sharp hooks
on each rig snag on
just about anything they touch.

The blue undersea the herring share
engages the blinding light.
Six herring appear, one on each hook.

With the sudden exposure to open air
revealed and naked
they wriggle, wildly silver.

Working the jigging line
not too high or hard,
just a slight movement, just a desire.

THREE FINGERED JACK

The day we hiked Three Fingered Jack
I was twenty, you were eighteen
the slopes beneath the rocky base
wind burned. The trail rose steeply
to an open moraine, then to a lofty point.
We reached the ridge top, the alpine range:
in the distance, the Three Sisters.

Above Jack's summit
we rested on the soaring rocky incline.
Bear grass grew below, tall feathers
sprang from an indigo lake.
Sheets of lava, igneous rock in our way
the crest of crags surrounded an abraded cone
an uneven volcano crimson with ebony bands.

When the sun moved below the horizon,
we were still high above on the trail.
Our breath and words appeared like clouds,
snow rested on ground cover,
the trail twisted and turned.
Chilled with fear we peered
into Jack's flinty face.

Along the narrow path
we inched our way through semi-darkness
to the meadow below. The year's low snowpack
had moved the peak bloom forward.
With joy we gazed at the meadow:
huckleberry, vanilla leaf, snowbrush
and salmonberry bloomed early.

FRANCE IN SEPTEMBER

That autumn I lived at L'Hotel De La Petite Fleur
in the old part of Nice, La Vieille Ville.
The room, four flights up,
a narrow winding staircase built during the Inquisition.
The walls a light brown Italian plaster.

I walked through the ancient streets
to the sun crested blue promenade
past a noisy market. Medieval gothic church
spires, stained glass: faces of saints
expressions of ecstasy.

Pigeons congregated
on the marble steps in sets of three;
siblings celebrating
a happy reunion,
exchanging the family news.

I met with friends in cafés
drank red wine through the afternoon
talked of plans to travel:
Greece in October
Spain in the spring.

I understood the French way of life
the passion of love and food
the intuitive voices echoing within.

Amelia Earhart in Heaven

I wake from a dream
about Amelia Earhart flying over the ocean.
Her airplane departed on the morning of July 2, 1937.
She arrived unknown to a secret island hidden
in the loneliness of the blue Pacific
below clouds and trees.

I doze on the wing of Amelia's airplane
powder blue sky peeks
through cumulus clouds.
Amelia accelerates, pistons crank furiously
rotate up and down, slap metal to metal
fire irregularly.

In my dream I fear falling from the wing
to the turquoise sea below
a plunge into a gem-hard surface.

Amelia walks fearless among the clouds
laughs about the myths she left behind,
wanders amidst silver stars.

To a Russian Poet

(Yevgeny Yevtushenko, 7/18/1932 to 4/1/2017)

I never met Yevtushenko
saw him read his poetry once
on David Frost. I remember watching
the flickering black and white TV transfixed.
Poets are revered in Russia.

Yevtushenko balanced carefully,
teetering on the top of the Berlin Wall between
East and West, between censorship and truth.
Faithful to his beliefs on writing and art
he traveled the Western world.

His most famous poem was "Babi Yar"
about the Nazi massacre of the Jewish population
in Kiev, 1941. The Soviets distorted the story,
claimed attacks on peaceful Soviet citizens,
covered up the anti-Semitic killing.

He loved America,
taught at the University of Tulsa.
In a 1995 AP interview, he praised his poetry students:
*sons of cowboys and oil engineers as more sensitive
because they didn't live in the big cities.*

Yevtushenko's grandfathers both
were imprisoned by Stalin
yet he carried the blazing flame of poetry
across the dark steppe, illuminating
Russia's frozen tundra.

Suffragettes March for Justice

A March morning cold and crisp on the third day
in 1913, women gather in the early hours
before the flaming orange sun rises
in the distance over the foggy D.C. city skyline.

Cady Stanton, Susan B. Anthony, Alice Paul arrive.
Inez Mulholland rides atop a white horse,
leading 5,000 Suffragettes down Pennsylvania Avenue.
They wear white, purple and green sashes:
white for purity, purple for loyalty and dignity, green for hope.

History has called them to stand and march
to raise their voices for the right to vote.
The clip-clop of horse's hooves during the early morning gathering
heard in the narrow streets, echoes like a clarion call.
Suffragettes left their children sleeping in beds,
their husbands sipping coffee at kitchen tables.

Suffragettes knew justice did not unfold
easily. It had to be pursued, forged
like a fine silver sword. Plunged into fire,
held under icy cold water, hammered
repeatedly, each flaw pounded out of the sterling metal.

Their lives had been forged
in the heat of protest, marches and speeches
frozen in the bitter cold during times
of loneliness, jail cells and exclusion.

They knew deep in their souls,
that justice was worth
the fight for women and all Americans.
To vote in the country they loved,
The 19th amendment embodied the right to life
to liberty and the pursuit of happiness.

BROWN LEATHER BOMBER JACKET

The zipper needed replacing,
the right pocket worn through
where my hand had rested.
Those times I stashed amber agates,
shells from the beach
in the pouch.

I bought the jacket for ninety dollars
at a small shop in Springfield,
fancied myself a young Amelia Earhart.
My jacket and a red tartan scarf
seemed dashing;
for twenty years it served me well.

My lover encouraged me to buy it.
She had several leather jackets of her own,
all different hues of black leather.
I brought it home,
enjoyed the crackle
of the metal zipper on rough leather.

Worn in all kinds of weather
my leather jacket is a second skin,
keeps me warm on winter nights
protects me on summer nights
girds the structure of my life
like the metaphors in a poem.

MOONLIGHT

We drive the highway to the next small town
the sun a white disc over your shoulder.
The red moon rises simultaneously
three herons glide on a stream of winter light.

Our conversation carries us over miles of open road
just before the moon takes her place
in the endless sky, the sanguine sun
departs with ravishing shades.

The herons stand in the winter mist
brave the dusk,
the road slopes upward, shoots
straight and wet across the valley.

Recognizing the moment,
we sketch scenes with our words,
search the horizon from the floating white sun
to the blazing red moon: confreres
they rise and set side by side.

Sacred Sauna

Daughter of the land,
the mountains and the trees
initiate passage again:
heat round rocks,
pour streams of mountain river water
on stones until they hiss and snap.

Steam rises from crimson,
blood rushes to your face, in a blush
mistrust, guilt, anger leave
through the opening
at the top of the sacred structure.

Our bodies drip sweat,
from your tan breast
a salty diamond lingers, suspended,
fire reflected in the single drop.
In conscious bliss, you begin
to whisper a woman's determination,
a ritual of compassion and courage.

San Felipe

You and I stretch out on a San Felipe beach
the curve of your back
slope of your thigh an endless continuation
of sun spangled slopes, our breasts whiter
than the fine grain sand on which we lie.

You rise, run, air spun in a moment
like an overabundant cherub.
I search the miles of aqua ocean
intent on seeing you on the horizon
with full intensity.

I turn to see your smile slide
into a glassy wave. You ascend again
like an ocean Madonna,
salty crystalline, dive, pierce
the turquoise blue sea.

Thigh slapping thigh, ribs drawn tightly
over shimmering skin, you run released,
skim liquid blue, collapse
like a desperate wild kite
kicking at the wind.

Motionless, we breathe
with the rhythm of the waves.
The ocean has seeped into your world
reflecting eyes, brilliant with
clear blue knowledge of the sea.

Your back coated with a million
tiny pieces of time
each reflecting its own sun:
our origin whispers over us
like a single silent gull.

Evening Prayer

Writing as a form of prayer
reading Thomas Merton's
The Seven Story Mountain late at night,
a record of Marvin Gaye in the background.

Today I left your apartment,
passing through rooms
above the garage; we made love
after a tense talk about where we are headed.

Feelings laid out like a place mat on the table,
you said you like the way I kiss
only a woman can kiss that way:
an interesting fact known to a small group of people.

Love and concern are etched lightly
on your radiant face.
What is your inclination tonight, perhaps
to purify ourselves ceremoniously?

Out the window seagulls call, dive,
tugboats red and white
navigate the waves.

Framed by the dark oak windowsill
the ocean mist begins to lift
revealing cliffs, seaweed, sandy beaches.

Yellow shards of morning sunlight
flash across the glass table top.
On the bed a folded note lies
on blue striped sheets.

Indian Summer

Late September morning
on the thirtieth day, day of my birth,
scarlet maple beckons.

Between my house and the street
this maple tree, gold tipped and crimson
ignites deep fired hopes
forged and burnished.

Leaves aflame with expectation
close at hand,
the maple flares, translucent,
life force awakens,
the day unfolds before me
without hesitation.

II.

Portland, the City

*I was a late bloomer, but anyone
who blooms at all, ever, is very lucky.*

—Sharon Olds

PULLING GREEN CHAIN
ON SAUVIE ISLAND, PORTLAND

Remember the summer we worked at Martin Brother's
Sawmill on Sauvie Island, up at dawn, the air frozen, frost
on the grass. Working on the green chain, sorting roofing
shingles, knotholes could be no larger than an inch in
diameter. A young guy, a blond boy biker with a crucifix
hanging from his right ear, worked side by side with me, his
jean jacket cut off at the shoulders. Working class kids and
college students home for the summer, we worked together.
On the other side of the mill, residents of the halfway
house for the mentally ill sorted shingles with vacant stares.
On our breaks: rushing out of the dark mill into the light,
laughing, shouting, grabbing peanut butter crackers, hot
chocolate from the dusty vending machine. We worked
until late in the afternoon. Tired, hungry we punched time
cards, hopped, skipped over sawdust covered planks.

early morning chill
shivering under blue jeans
look east to the sun

Portland Rail Yard

The lime-bitter wind
buffets the young traveler as he hops
over the rusty rims of the railroad track.

Cobwebs in the freight car shimmer
like constellations surging in the noir night
bandied about by gusts and breezes.

The next morning, a flaming sun springs along the horizon
reflecting on yellow fields and more green fields beyond,
red clay woven into the hard railroad ground.

Houses, signposts, roads, flash by swiftly
like images in a film clip, a flock of blackbirds
rest in a copse near a thicket of small tree shoots.

The traveler grabs his knapsack, jumps off the freight train,
rolls into a lush maze of corn, chasing a dream.
Fields throw off tender light.

Freight Train, Eugene to Portland

It occurred to me during the Fall of 1982 riding a freight
train from Eugene to Portland with my girlfriend Kate
that anyone who was an English major at an American
university had read *On the Road* by Jack Kerouac. We hide
between two shabby freight cars, graffiti covering the doors,
wait for our chance. The railroad engineer has just passed
on his rounds. We climb the thin metal rungs of the train
ladder, jump into the freight car, huddle together as the
wagon lurches and jerks forward, north toward Portland.
In the afternoon, red and orange leaves blow across the
silver plated tracks. The scent of autumn smoke lingers in
the brisk air, sun beams down from the powder blue sky.
We hear the steady rhythm of railroad cars clicking over
the tracks.

St. Jack's September Midnight

—after Jack Kerouac's Desolation Angels

Down from Desolation Peak after sixty-three days on the
Fire Lookout at Skagit Valley, Washington he hitched to
Seattle, bought a bottle of Christian Brother's port, hopped
a freight from the coast down to San Francisco to his first
bountiful dinner in Chinatown. At Desolation Peak he had
come face to face with the unfathomable void, surpassing
peace, surpassing gratification, surpassing joy. He had
arrived at the San Francisco Poetry Renaissance. French
Canadian, Catholic, Buddhist, he saw the somber hidden
wings on all humanity, each one a Buddha.

September midnight
one low cloud passes quickly
moonlight on his face

Timber Town

Pacific currents along the ocean coast
high tides surge
touched by Chinook winds.
Gold wheat rolls
farmland ripples,
dark loam fields surround red barns.

The timberline stretches beyond
homestead boundaries,
weather-stained farm buildings.
Cabin windows light up at dinner time
logs depart downstream, rivers muddied,
above, rain soaked peaks and misty summits.

Logging early mornings along the coast
working a few miles from mill towns
in the coast range, loggers
sawmill workers, road crews
gather after quitting time
at the Bayside Bar and Grill.

Some survived World War II, some Vietnam.
Glad at the end of another workday
they raise amber pints between the pool table
and the bar, trade logging stories,
shake mud off calk boots, joke about
getting home to a warm fire, a hot meal.

SISTER MARY FRANCES

Sister Mary Frances fell asleep in grace
and redemption, a nun for sixty-four years.
She had a great love and appreciation
for the kindness shown by parishioners.
Taking the religious vow of poverty
she moved to an ocean-side village,
entered the Hermitage of Our Lady of the Sea.

The Hermitage was founded
by Sister Mary Benedict
with whom she shared the hermit's life
for the rest of her years.
Her life's motto, to praise, to bless, to teach.
The gold cross and ring she wore
her only earthly possessions.

Grade School Champs

We won the city championship that year at Richmond
Grade School in Portland, Richmond written in gold
cursive script across our royal blue t-shirts. Girls' basketball
in 1968, Mr. Wong was our coach. The youngest on the
team, I admired the older eighth grade girls Shelly and
Dory, both pegged their levis skin tight. We could only
dribble three times, we had to pass the ball, couldn't cross
the center-line, it was half court. Three teammates on each
side, one rover. I was five foot nine, a gangly twelve-year-
old. We were much hardier than they thought. We all lined
up with the girls' basketball trophy at the end of the season.
In the local newspaper photo, our hands held the golden
figure, a basketball player perched high on a pedestal: she
aimed the ball, arched her back, ready to sink a basket.

looking for the pass
dashing quick across the court
the ball stings my hands

Yellowknife

As a young man my father mined gold in Yellowknife,
he described yellow flakes layered in black rock,
told stories about the Wildcat Café.
First opened in 1937, miners found women and whiskey
at the Gold Nugget Bar, some men never left,
worked in the mine all week,
lost at cards, unlucky in life and games of chance.

Yellowknife named for the Yellowknife Indians
the Copper Indians.
Near the Arctic coast,
the Yellowknife Indians traded tools
made from copper deposits.

Steep mountains in the Yukon Territory
filled with vast rivers.
Grizzly bears and wolves wander
through forests of spruce and birch
the landscape scoured by wind
rolling areas of bare stone
grey rock among patches of lichen.

My father talked about endless lakes, the big lake,
Great Slave Lake, surrounded by several small lakes.
The high latitude of Yellowknife caused
variations between night and day:
twenty hours of darkness in December,
twilight lasted all night in June.

He saved his weekly pay,
collected gold dust in a small aspirin bottle.
His bunk-mate was a member of the Yellowknife tribe.
They became good friends, didn't talk much
but trusted each other
when mining deep below the earth.

A Day at Rockaway Beach

My little sisters and I
walk along the shoreline
in the direction of the rose-hued sun
as surf pounds inland. We skip
through shifting drifts, shadows
from our shovels, pails, waver large on the dunes.

Shells collected for our sand castle
arranged around a small turret,
toy boats float in the castle moat,
south wind grazes our backs.
Blue striped beach umbrellas scattered
along the shoreline.

The scent of brine in the seaweed air,
a ship glints on the horizon
red and white buoys bob near the reef
a warning to all fishing boats.
I look toward the waves, run, splash in the swell,
red shorts, bare chest, blond.

Under a beach umbrella
mother spots the rolling log in the surf.
Terrified, she screams *run, run.*
Dad hoists me up with one arm, outruns the log.
Multi-colored points of light
flash across the ocean.

After a picnic lunch, Dad talks
about the danger of rolling logs,
sneaker waves. My sisters and I etch our names
in white sand with driftwood sticks.
Without a care, across the surf
sand-cranes skitter.

PIANOFORTE

On my way back to the office after lunch
I spot a yellow piano
on the sidewalk on Second Street.
It stands idling like a shiny yellow taxi.
Pulling the bench forward,
I place my hands on the ivory keys.

I'm transported back to piano lessons in fourth grade.
Mrs. Little, my Irish Catholic piano teacher, spry at eighty years,
her bright copper hair encased in a net,
her cheeks dusted with pink powder
a string of white pearls dangling
from her ancient neck.
She attends Mass in the very early mornings.

Two grand pianos grace her living room,
two uprights fill her dining room.
I practice Bach and Beethoven for recitals,
my mouth firmly set, my eyes darting across the keys
counting beats and measures, the metronome keeping time.

My parents' working wages, hard won,
they requested songs they would recognize.
I began to practice
songs from Broadway plays,
Fiddler on the Roof,
Oklahoma, West Side Story.

On Second Street, the high summer sun
shines a spotlight down on the yellow piano.
Bach and Beethoven please some sidewalk strollers,
for fans of Broadway musicals
my repertoire includes, "If I Were a Rich Man," "Maria,"
and "The Surrey with the Fringe on Top."

VITTORIO

When I was almost nine, I rode my
ten speed bike through a Portland neighborhood
past white clapboard houses row after row
to the little mom and pop grocery store on the corner.
Parked my luminous steed without a lock
outside the swinging doors.

Dashing out of the store
with my ice cream sandwich in hand
my bike left leaning against
the lamppost was gone.

The brilliant metallic blue,
the U-shaped handlebars
formed like the horns of a wild ram.
The Italian brand, Vittorio, stamped on the frame,
a regal lion roaring, mouth open, red tongue
surrounded by a royal Italian crest,
circled with olive branches.

Who took my bike, a birthday gift I was proud of?
Vaporized, disappeared, it left a mark,
like a slap on the face, hot and red.
I walked the blacktop streets in southeast Portland
looking for the leather saddle, looking for the
U-shaped handle bars, the gleaming majestic blue.

PIERI'S RISTORANTE

Pieri's was located on 39th Ave. in Portland,
the scent of hot peppers, dry Italian salami,
garlic, and pepperoni filled the air
when we walked through the door.

A glass case full of cream filled Italian pastries,
bottles of red wine, Frascatis and Chianti's lined the walls
from ceiling to floor. An Italian flag draped overhead,
minestrone soup in glass gallon containers on the counter.

Pieri welcomed us, invited us in,
leaned over the counter
his dark hair combed back,
pencil thin mustache above his lip.

His white shirt pressed, dark slacks creased,
an apron string strung around his waist,
a chain with a holy medal hung from his neck,
a photo of him in Italy captured his youth.

We ordered Italian pizza with hot peppers,
the thin crust cut into small squares rather than triangles,
rich marinara sauce laden
with spicy green peppers and real pepperoni.

When I returned from college to my hometown,
Pieri's was gone, a 7-Eleven had taken its place.

Butterfly Sanctuary, Portland Arboretum

A butterfly like a leaf falls from a tree,
rising, falling, dipping over and over.
We grasp at the enormous air
a red and pink butterfly lands gently on your shoulder,
today we live, fly with the freedom of Papillion.

Sixty hungry caterpillars mark the end
of a breeding season by conservationists:
the Oregon Silver-spot is released
to the slopes of Mt. Hebo.

Butterflies surround us like bright colored confetti,
Summer at the butterfly lab,
3,000 butterflies fly into the forests
of Oregon and Washington.

Two small Admiral butterflies red and black
sail and circle each other,
drink from the water of a mountain stream
and float into the trees.

We discover the Taylor's Checker Spot butterfly
endangered and under review for federal listing.
Across the world cultures view the butterfly
as an image of hope, endurance, change.

The Great Purple Emperor, deep violet
flies with joy, granter of wishes,
the symbol of life.
transforming color, changing luck.

As we turn, a Blue Monarch flies by,
its colors range from stark indigo to powder blue
with touches of dark black
at the edge of each wing.

A large vibrant Orange Monarch
lands near you on a blade of grass, flutters her wings
causes the wind to blow, storms to rage
in September in the deep Amazon forests of Peru.

On the wall, behind the half-filled amber bottles:
John Fitzgerald Kennedy,
Edward Moore Kennedy,
a picture of Pope John Paul the second,
a restoration of Vatican II and the Latin liturgy.

The penny whistle slides forth and back,
coasts over green hills,
rocky slopes of County Clare,
County Kilkenny, County Cork.

My childhood friend Sylvia plays her guitar with authority
her silver hair wild, glints like a Celtic specter
her musical partner Lance on a dulcimer
pounds out "Old Joe Clark" like a step dancer on a stage
or a writer drawing out a metaphor.

Pints quench a Saturday night thirst.
Families with children and minors can stay until 9:00 pm.
The barmaid with dark hair,
beauty behind black frames and thick lenses, says
we sweep them out at 9:00 p.m.
The working man beside me asks
how much I'll pay him to save my seat.
Barstool bold, he intends to drink all night.

Through the door my sister and niece arrive
like Gaelic visions come to greet me.
We find a nook by the dartboard to listen
to the lilting tunes,
the sterling poetry of Irish history.

BLACK BEAR

The black bear wanders into town.
First spotted in Ferguson's yard
and again at the Mitchel's, by the red garden shed.
No one seems upset by his presence.
McCarty dashes into his house
finds his binoculars in the bedroom dresser drawer.

We wait, patiently taking turns with the binoculars.
I notice details of the bear's winter coat,
thick with red tones, his huge claws,
curved two inches from his toes.

We observe the bear brush up against the fence
amble across the meadow in Legacy Park
back up through the white yarrow
and blue morning glories
into the stand of Douglas Firs
behind Max O'Brien's cottage.

I think of the other bears up in the hills
above the valley, less to sustain them,
few provisions from which to forage.
I know I'll see this bear again next spring.
McCarty hears his wife call over the fence
gives a shrug, turns and leaves through the gate.

I look up: overhead, wave after wave
of Canadian geese honk, fly
in an audible rippling formation,
calling to each other, anxiously.

Powell's Bookstore

While perusing the poetry section
at Powell's, suddenly blaring from the loudspeaker:
Attention: Larry Leiderman please come
to the Blue Room to be reunited with your wife.
I imagine Larry Leiderman picking up a book on happiness
by the Dalai Lama or a copy of the spiritual writings of Rumi.

I envision Larry Leiderman leaning against a bookshelf
wandering through aisles and aisles of books
to the biographies. I see Larry Leiderman immersed
in flipping through the early life of Calvin Coolidge
one of our most laconic presidents
or perhaps skimming a volume of Auden's life and poetry.

Does Larry Leiderman want to be reunited
with his wife? Maybe he's joyfully
reading Jung's *Dreams* in the Rose Room
or having a cup of coffee and a scone in the café
with a copy of D.H. Lawrence.
Perhaps he's picked up *The Sheltering Sky* by Paul Bowles
or imagines himself sailing across Jean Rhys's *Wide Sargasso Sea.*

St. David of Wales Church, Portland

—after William Carlos Williams' "The Catholic Bells"

My mother was Anglican, Church of England
my father Catholic, Church of Rome.
Though I'm no Anglican nor Catholic
the red brick steeple, the bright red arched doorway
of St. David of Wales Episcopal Church
beckons me on Sunday morning.

The young priest, Father James
rushes to early morning Mass
dressed in priestly robes of purple and gold.
His thin frame, deep-set eyes define him.
At the coffee reception after the service
he chats with parishioners, glances
over the dark frames of his glasses,
adjusts his white collar.

The psalms and sermon earlier,
cast sparks of inspiration through the parish.
The droll angle of the sanctuary
seen from the church pews
accentuated his stark profile.
The Sunday sermon alleviates
the drudgery of the week,
elevates the aspirations of all.

Those in the parish pray for peace
greet one another
with *peace be with you.*
All are ready to embark into the world again,
to return to their homes with a little hope.

The bells of St. David's ring out,
announce a wedding, a baptism, a birth.
The bells peal again and again
across Portland neighborhoods
over the wide porches and green window frames
of the well-kept clapboard houses.

The Old Masonic Cemetery

I forge my way from the bottom of the hill past overgrown ferns, green weeds, yellow dandelions, and puffs. The worn gravestones scattered lonely on the side of the paths, a hot day in July, stop on the trail, drink deeply from my water bottle. The city founders buried here. On the other side of the hill, on the downward slope, the mausoleum stands, built of solid white stone, an Egyptian motif, a pharaoh and a winged dog guard the arched doorway. Steel bars prevent anyone from leaving or entering.

honeybee flies past
close to my ear, glad buzzing
wildflowers blooming

Lunch with Anne

Overlooking the Clackamas River
we meet for lunch at the Amber Lodge,
built with charred logs.
On the serpentine river below
two figures float on colorful pontoons.

We order chilled white wine,
this lodge known for its salmon
that swim and struggle up the river rapids.
Birds circle; you look up
with curiosity, fear:
are they crows or gulls?
Sunlight shines on us, hot, sharp, shafts.
We move toward fragments of shade.

Our friendship transcends time,
we talk of the past, when we were moored
at other rivers, lakes and streams.
Memories drift with us out to sea.
Another glass of wine and chocolate mousse
offset our worries about life and death.

Your beauty is reflected in your summer blue eyes
the color unchanged since we were twenty.
You've now immersed yourself in ocean depths
to face the last of Buddhism's four sufferings:
birth, sickness, old age, death.

Your sense of humor still intact
you bravely fight on, not giving in
to the predictions of godlike entities
who leave out hope and love.
Your damn belligerence
extends your life,
you will never go quietly.

Messages of Peace in the Sky

The blue rain bends the Japanese maples
towards blades of jade grass.
This morning your smile
was left in the breakfast nook.
The warmth of your voice
now embraces me like amber honey
with hope and a vision of March and Spring.

Out my kitchen window
kites with colorful tails kick up their heels
in the wind above the treetops
fly soulfully to the top of purple Mount Fuji
become midnight stars.
White messages of peace in the indigo blue sky
beyond my backyard.

—after Elizabeth Bishop's "The Map"

I reach into the glove box for the map,
eight creased sections unfurl
like an accordion
ripple over the dashboard.
Across mountains black lines climb,
red lines snake through foothills
along the Cascade Range.

Blue shade represents changes in elevation
pale green indicates the hills, acres of Douglas Fir.
Yellow notations are for Idaho and Washington
with California at the border.
Purple highlights national parks like Crater Lake,
tan identifies Warm Springs, the Cayuse Indian Reservation.
The deeper blue reveals rivers, lakes, tributaries.

My map guides me to the tiny town of Glendale
three hours south, population eight hundred,
high above in the mountains.
With no public library in town, I meet my counseling client
in a quiet corner of the Morning Star Café.
After two hours and two mochas,
our interview is complete.

On the way home, my map leads me
through small towns off Highway I-5:
Canyonville, home of Seven Feathers Casino
and the Cow Creek band of Umpqua Indians.
A turquoise inlay surrounds the casino windows
like stones in the necklace of a Native woman;
at the entrance a seven-foot eagle
carved in cedar dives for salmon.

As the sun sets, I drive into Myrtle Creek,
where time stopped in 1940.
The road leads past a faded Coke sign
paint chipped on the side of an old red brick building.
Kids on bikes scatter under a railroad bridge,
a yellow dog runs behind.

Crossing the Burnside Bridge

Remember how I used to talk about Portland,
about walking over the Burnside Bridge,
the Willamette River swirling far below,
sailboats, tugboats, vying for position on the river.
The 1920 bridge architecture, two turrets, a watchman
surveying the river for the great ships.
Walking into old town, White Stag sign hovering over it all,
today we cross the bridge, walk for justice.

When we were kids we picked strawberries,
raspberries in fields just outside of Portland,
earned enough to buy school clothes in the fall.
Burnside on the other side of the bridge was known as skid row,
our berry bus, a rusty yellow school bus
stopped to pick up the winos from Burnside.
They picked berries alongside us, their tokay bottles
lined the rows of strawberry fields.

Pendleton Mill store windows
displayed blue-collar work clothes, heavy plaid shirts
red and yellow wool blankets adorned with teepees,
solid leather work boots, all beckoned the day laborer.
We walked west past St. Andre's Catholic mission,
past the dimly lit bars, dark dives, pink neon signs,
Mary's strip club, the Paris theatre,
hard-core porn shown all night long.

We walked to China Town to Hung Far Low's
known for the best chop suey and mai-tais,
past the Jazz De Opus, bean bag chairs,
strong cheap drinks, primo jazz club.
Past Powell's Book Store, titles in the window
A Portrait of the Artist as a Young Man, Our Lady of the Flowers by Genet.
A walk further up to Washington Park, a statue of Sacajawea
pointed the way to the Lewis and Clark trail.

Now we cross the Burnside Bridge,
we protest in the pulsing heat of 2020,
vibrant stars clamor, sway about the moon.
To the east seven mountain peaks cluster
around Mt. Hood. This burning August we march for justice,
we write, we sing, we dance, we claim the
summer. It echoes over the Burnside Bridge,
through the streets and buildings of the holy night.

III.

Love and Transformation

*The main thing is to be moved,
to love, to tremble, to live.*

—Auguste Rodin

BEACH CAMPING

Last night camping in my car, the back seat folded down. I
gaze up at sterling-plated stars. Dozing, dreaming, the light
eases into morning, waves crash rhythmically on the beach.
Soon the sun streams in, golden bars of morning light.
Out the car window, seals sprawl across barnacled rocks.
I snuggle further into the down sleeping bag, think about
your kiss; it took me by surprise when you leaned in for our
usual hug; now the entire summer is spread out before us.

summer sun warms us
in the wildflower meadow
purple crocus blooms

DIMANCHE

In Paris they kiss in the streets:
you said we were on the wrong continent.
I had to agree.

Our day began chanting the sutra,
coffee at Cafe Nicoise,
we spoke broken French.

Later, out for a drink,
a glass of chablis blanc at the gay bar.
The waitress filled our glasses to the brim.

The city was ours.
An early dinner, mushrooms, calamari
red wine, a walk down the boulevard.

Before you left, we kissed hard in the street.
As I looked up, a bird faded into clouds.

Blue Star, White Star

You sleep soundly
breathe deep and even.
White star falling,
your parted lips, reflect gold light.

Planets flash among constellations.
Out the window a passing flight
from the dark sky arches down to earth.
I think about waking you.

Orion the hunter appears, easily recognized.
A blue, white star rends
the midnight sky.
Rapture summons us
from the firmament of the heavens.

REFLECTIONS AFTER THE FACT

Past wild birches, on the road where you live,
a house up the mountain.
Paths, hedges, walkways before us,
a meadow circles your hillside home.
In the moon's dark phases
an act of surrender.

Your uncanny enticement,
I ask for another glass of Syrah.
Hidden away from the public,
we watch a colony of wild turkeys
run sprightly through maple trees.
Later, a family of deer surveys us with wide eyes.

The night has left us rising
like seraphim, floating into the vapors.
This is no time to be alone.
Jagged rocks and smooth stones
surround your house like fallen men
curled up tightly against the advancing storm.

The World Sails Away
Beyond My Backyard

The dog in the yard next door barks incessantly
as I wait for your phone call.
You asked me to call each day
but no calls now. Are we breaking up
in the middle of a pandemic?

Neighbors think nothing has changed;
they go about their daily routine.
I stay inside except to buy groceries, pick up the mail,
working remotely with one client,
pretend it's enough.

Each new day begins with coffee, meditation,
National Public Radio in the morning.
I hang my clothes to dry on the back deck
while a blue bird on the fence supervises.
I promise myself to continue writing each day.

In the kitchen a steaming pot of soup simmers,
the dog next door continues to bark
the world sails along beyond my backyard.
All assumptions about my life fly outward
into the endless stratosphere.

LENTIL SOUP

When I make my special lentil soup,
the scent of garlic
flows throughout the house, steam rising.
The hardy soup cooked to perfection:
lentils savory in a bowl from Greece or Saudi Arabia.

Best of all the vegetables, carrots, celery,
onions compliment each other
sautéed in butter, garlic and black pepper.

A thick piece of crusty bread
sliced with a knife, a wedge of sharp cheddar
all swallowed down
with a glass of cold white wine.

In a short while I'll go up to bed
fall into the down comforter,
beneath flannel sheets, satisfied.
Contentment arrives in the night.

Cherry Tree

I look up from my coffee mug
at the cherries hanging from the tree in the backyard:
red, plump, bursting with sweetness, too high to reach,
so much abundance out of range.

We've been alone now for months.
It's June, our relationship on hold
and may be over, each day slipping by
like a bird flying east.

Cherries hang from branches
ready to eat. Blue jays, squirrels
raccoons gather together in the tree
to savor the over-ripe fruit.

We wait until it's safe; we wait in expectation
to know for sure the time is right.
Until then, only squirrels and blue jays
enjoy the cherries in the cherry tree.

Life Lesson

The orange feral cat in the backyard
sits smartly between
yellow daffodils and red roses.
She blinks at me through the window
as I wash the dinner dishes.

Her tail wrapped snuggly around her feet,
patient, she's a living entity, a sentient being.
I'm glad to see her
life pulsing around her, electric
like a Van Gogh painting.

The orange tabby seems to implore
that I be the one to forgive first.
Love asks us to expand our lives,
to increase our capacity to live
in the current moment, to let the past go.

This late afternoon in August, the sun shines
far too bright in my blue-grey eyes.
Through the kitchen window
I watch yew trees float in the wind,
lush green branches waving invitation.

Sappho on a Clay Vase

—after Rainer Maria Rilke's "Alcestis"

Sappho embraces her poet lover Eranna. They rise above an
angry exchange with a male adversary, slip on their sandals,
walk from under the yew tree to greener paths in the hills
of Lesbos. They know their love will endure: they have
escaped the male gaze, they fit together like a lid on a bowl.
Sappho and Eranna immerse themselves in art, leave all
distractions behind.

the brave burro climbs
up the gorge of the mountain
with a load of figs

Before the Wildfires

She wrote the phone number
hastily on the palm of her hand.
Rode home hard and fast on her lucky bike.
The number partially disappeared
with the hot sweat of her palm.

She dashed into the house
copied the number on a grocery receipt.
Wind began to bang against the house:
a warning that trees and power lines could be down
in the coming days.

Her lights flickered;
the living room lost electricity.
Under the last low light,
she looked at the number again.
She wanted to think
about the phone number
alone in the dark.

Navigation Among the Riptides

—after "To the Harbormaster" by Frank O'Hara

Lover, you are a boat tossed
on tempestuous seas
barely avoiding a shiver of sharks.
The waves too high to hold you,
I rotate the windlass, throw the anchor out,
hurl a lanyard to moor you, look to starboard,
you, a sailing ship riding through rough gales.

Fierce winds blow, tossed by swells,
your topsail unfurled, white foam
drenches your deck over the bulwark.
With a lunge and a thrust I try
to navigate the sweeping surges
but the dawn of wild winds
pounds rolling pathways.

Approaching a rocky formation,
the sea filled with ridges rising from green waters,
faint sunlight through angry grey clouds is the sole
   restoration.
You clamber into a cove of monstrous rocks
the riptide crashes, infusing tension:
finally separation into
the dying day.

Writer at Work

How do we defeat the plague? Through common decency.
—Albert Camus, The Plague

Enforced writing retreat
months of disciplined
revising and re-envisioning each day.

Alone with her muse,
a writer's loneliness,
she endures painful isolation.

Early summer love affair, nights of anguish
marked by self-interrogation
and uncertainty.

Hiking along the riverbank, a precipitous climb,
rougher terrain than I recall: the cost demanded
by a love that didn't work out.

My worries have always
brought out my best qualities: the secret,
unleashed desire.

Sitting down to write
everything here on earth is before me,
no wandering among distant planets.

Just a writer leading an ordinary life,
evoking changes in the rhythm of the tides,
and the waxing and waning of the moon.

Embracing the Northern Light

—after "Dance Russe" by William Carlos Williams

The neighborhood is slumbering.
The moon a dazzling white crescent floats
brazenly above empty lots, woods and fields
in the small hours of morning.

Overhead, flashing stars streak,
lighting up shadows of sober Douglas firs.
These trees were confidents and friends of my youth.
From my simple rooms I rise early
and begin to chant the sutra.

Chanting alone I face east
look at my strong hands and tan arms,
sing quietly *I am not afraid, I am not afraid,*
I will stand firm, at one with myself.

Against the rose crested dawn
of this Milky Way morning,
light seeps through the window blinds.
I continue to chant and sing,
the hardy optimist
in this clapboard house.

POETRY WRITING, 101

In my teaching years, I prepared Thursday nights
for my 6–8:00 p.m. class.
Traffic picked up in the streets
often stuck idling at the railroad tracks, waiting for the train to pass.
Rain, clear sky as I approach the classroom;
expectant students waiting, eager.
We began by sharing poems
from poets they especially like, who inspire them:
passions rise, the written word promises
awakenings, mysteries.

Intelligence, curiosity in their wild eyes,
they expect wise words.
I turn the discussion back to each student
the class unfolds, discourse begins.
Students, young at twenty,
one student in her eighties,
a few teachers have signed up
who want to learn to teach poetry.

We study the villanelles of Dylan Thomas
the images of William Carlos Williams,
the metaphors of Sylvia Plath.
I entreat them to travel to the country of poetry,
explore its rolling rivers, rocky deserts.
They take a poem, ravish it like a hungry lover.

At the Hong Kong restaurant after class,
I sit alone, a back table
where I'm able to see the entire dining room.
I order a cold glass of chablis
a steaming plate of chicken chow yuk, hot oil on the side,
the egg rolls with plum sauce arrive.
While I wait for the main dish,
I realize loss is a hallmark of identity.
We don't have to reclaim everything.

Acknowledgments

Grateful acknowledgment is made to the editors of the following poetry journals and anthologies in which these poems or earlier versions of them first appeared.

Third Wednesday, A Literary & Arts Journal:
"The Old Masonic Cemetery"

San Pedro River Review: "Fishing for Herring"

Timberline Review: "Dimanche"

CIRQUE: A Literary Journal for the North Pacific Rim:
"Freight Train, Eugene to Portland"

Red River Review: "France in September"

Pandemic Puzzle Poems Anthology (Blue Light Press):
"Lentil Soup," "Before the Wildfires"

It Demands a Wildness of Me Anthology (Uttered Chaos Press): "County Cork Public House, Portland," "The Black Bear," "Vittorio"

Her Flag Art Project, Artist, Marylin Artus Oregon State Capital Galleria, 100 Anniversary of the 19thAmendment, February 2020: "Suffragettes March for Justice"

Digging Eclectic Anthology (Eliza Press): "Gargoyle"

Completion, Compilation Anthology (Eliza Press):
"Indian Summer," "Evening Prayer," "Sacred Sauna," "Young Woman Sage," "Moonlight"

Her-Story Anthology (Eliza Press): "The Dashboard Saint"

Songs of Ourselves Poetry Anthology (SGI Friends): "Messages of Peace in the Sky"

Janice D. Rubin is a counselor and educator. She received her M.S. from the University of Oregon and her B.A. in English Literature. Her work has appeared in *Third Wednesday, Literary & Arts Journal, San Pedro River Review, The Timberline Review, Red River Review, Cirque, a Literary Journal for the North Pacific Rim, Tiger's Eye Journal, Glass: A Journal of Poetry,* the *Austin International Poetry Anthology, It Demands a Wildness of Me* Poetry Anthology (Uttered Chaos Press), and *Pandemic Puzzle Poems Anthology* (Blue Light Press) among others. She was nominated for the Pushcart Poetry Prize in 2008. In 2017, she was a finalist for the Blue Light Press Book Award. In 2019, her book *Tin Coyote* was nominated for the Stafford/Hall Award for Poetry. She has taught at Oregon State University and Lane Community College. She's the author of *Transcending Damnation Creek Trail & Other Poems* (Flutter Press, 2010) and *Tin Coyote* (Blue Light Press, 2018). *Crossing the Burnside Bridge & Other Poems* is her third collection of poetry.

About Cirque Press

Cirque Press grew out of *Cirque*, a literary journal that publishes the works of writers and artists from the North Pacific Rim, a region that reaches north from Oregon to the Yukon Territory, south through Alaska to Hawaii, and west to the Russian Far East.

Cirque Press is a partnership of Sandra Kleven, publisher, and Michael Burwell, editor. Ten years ago, we recognized that works of talented writers in the region were going unpublished, and the Press was launched to bring those works to fruition. We publish fiction, nonfiction, and poetry, and we seek to produce art that provides a deeper understanding about the region and its cultures. The writing of our authors is significant, personal, and strong.

Sandra Kleven – Michael Burwell, publishers and editors
www.cirquejournal.com

Apportioning the Light by Karen Tschannen (2018)

The Lure of Impermanence by Carey Taylor (2018)

Echolocation by Kristin Berger (2018)

Like Painted Kites & Collected Works by Clifton Bates (2019)

Athabaskan Fractal: Poems of the Far North
by Karla Linn Merrifield (2019)

Holy Ghost Town by Tim Sherry (2019)

Drunk on Love: Twelve Stories to Savor Responsibly
by Kerry Dean Feldman (2019)

Wide Open Eyes: Surfacing from Vietnam
by Paul Kirk Haeder (2020)

Silty Water People by Vivian Faith Prescott (2020)

Life Revised by Leah Stenson (2020)

Oasis Earth: Planet in Peril by Rick Steiner (2020)

The Way to Gaamaak Cove by Doug Pope (2020)

Loggers Don't Make Love by Dave Rowan (2020)

The Dream That Is Childhood by Sandra Wassilie (2020)

Seward Soundboard by Sean Ulman (2020)

The Fox Boy by Gretchen Brinck (2021)

Lily Is Leaving: Poems by Leslie Ann Fried (2021)

One Headlight by Matt Caprioli (2021)

November Reconsidered by Marc Janssen (2021)

Callie Comes of Age by Dale Champlin (2021)

Someday I'll Miss This Place Too by Dan Branch (2021)

Out There In The Out There by Jerry McDonnell (2021)

Fish the Dead Water Hard by Eric Heyne (2021)

Salt & Roses by Buffy McKay (2022)

Growing Older In This Place: A Life in Alaska's Rainforest
by Margo Wasserman Waring (2022)

Kettle Dance: A Big Sky Murder by Kerry Dean Feldman (2022)

Nothing Got Broke by Larry F. Slonaker (2022)

On the Beach: Poems 2016-2021 by Alan Weltzien (2022)

Sky Changes on the Kuskokwim by Clifton Bates (2022)

Transplanted by Birgit Lennertz Sarrimanolis (2022)

Between Promise and Sadness by Joanne Townsend (2022)

Yosemite Dawning by Shauna Potocky (2022)

The Woman Within by Tami Phelps and
Kerry Dean Feldman (2023)

In the Winter of the Orange Snow by Diane S. Carpenter (2023)

Mail Order Nurse by Sue Lium (2023)

All in Due Time by Kate Troll (2023)

*Infinite Meditations For Inspiration and Daily
Practice* by Scott Hanson (2023)

Getting Home from Here by Anne Ward-Masterson (2023)

Crossing the Burnside Bridge & Other Poems
by Janice D. Rubin (2023)

*May the Owl Call Again: A Return to Poet John Meade
Haines, 1924–2011* by Rachel Epstein (2023)

CIRCLES *Illustrated books from Cirque Press*

Baby Abe: A Lullaby for Lincoln by Ann Chandonnet (2021)

Miss Tami, Is Today Tomorrow? by Tami Phelps (2021)

Miss Bebe Goes to America by Lynda Humphrey (2022)

www.ingramcontent.com/pod-product-compliance
Lightning Source LLC
Chambersburg PA
CBHW070918160726

48004CB00003B/1416